Quips and Quotes

Vol. 3 -

Patriots, Politicians and Pundits

Compiled by Dave Smith

Most of the material in this book has been compiled over a long period of time. Where the source is known, it is listed.

Published by:

Spring Ridge Publishing
P.O. Box 3301
Gainesville, GA 30503
United States of America

ISBN: 1470089157, 978-1470089153

Introduction copyright © 2012 Dave Smith

Other books by Dave Smith:

Quips, Quotes and Funnies, Vol. 1
Quips and Quotes, Vol. 2, Leadership
Growing Up Southern Style

Dedicated to the men and women who have served in the military to preserve the America we love.

CONTENTS

Introduction

When I started my research for Volume 3 of the Quips and Quotes series, I thought it would just be another interesting collection of thoughts for just another little book. Boy, was I in for a real awakening!

The more I read, the more I researched, the more I realized that I couldn't just list a bunch of "one-liners" and be done with it.

As I began to look at the repetitive themes and clear opinions of the great thinkers and founders of our nation, it was obvious that this would have to be a collection that includes longer segments to get the full sense of their meaning.

For example, the quote from Thomas Jefferson about a "wall of separation" between church and state is so obviously taken out of context.

The entire text clearly talks about restrictions on the *legislature*. It is obviously intended to reassure the members of the Danbury Baptist Association that they have nothing to fear from the government.

Of curious interest is Jefferson's clear distrust for the Supreme Court. He repeatedly expressed frustration over the court in letters. It makes one wonder how a contemporary court would twist Jefferson's words and intent to create something never mentioned in the constitution.

Jefferson would roll over in his grave.

It may come as no surprise to you that the longest section is "Liberty." The founders held the concept in such high esteem – and we seem to take it so much for granted!

Unless absolutely necessary to clarify meaning, I've avoided editing archaic language. In those few instances that are edited, the original words are intact and clearer, more modern terminology is in brackets.

In a few cases, I've found contemporary quotes of "pundits and politicians" that stand in stark opposition to the words and thoughts of the founders (the patriots).

Take some time and enjoy the collection. You will be surprised, amused and inspired by the writings of some great and a few not-so-great characters of history.

Dave Smith

CHARACTER

It's great to be great, but it's better to be human.

    - Will Rogers

I pronounce it as certain that there was never yet a truly great man that was not at the same time truly virtuous.

        - Ben Franklin, The Busy-body, No. 3, 1728

Enlightened statesmen will not always be at the helm.

        - James Madison, Federalist No. 10, 1787

It is of great importance to set a resolution...never to tell an untruth. There is no vice so mean, so pitiful, so contemptible; and he who permits himself to tell a lie once, finds it much easier to do it a second and a third time, till at length it becomes habitual; he tells lies without attending to it, and truths without the world believing him.
> - Thomas Jefferson, Letter to Peter Carr, 1785

[He] will live in the memory and gratitude of the wise & good, as a luminary of science, as a votary of liberty, as a model of patriotism, and as a benefactor of human kind.
> - James Madison, on Thomas Jefferson in a letter to Nicholas P. Trist, 1826

A spoonful of honey will catch more flies than a gallon of vinegar.
> - Ben Franklin, Poor Richard's Almanac, 1748

He was certainly one of the most learned men of the age. It may be said of him as has been said of others that he was a "walking Library," and what can be said of but few such prodigies, that the Genius of Philosophy ever walked hand in hand with him.

- James Madison, On Thomas Jefferson - letter to Samuel Harrison Smith, 1826

His temper was excellent, and he generally observed decorum in debate. On one or two occasions I have seen him angry, and his anger was terrible; those who witnessed it, were not disposed to rouse it again.

- Thomas Jefferson, About Patrick Henry, December, 1824

I Pray Heaven to Bestow The Best of Blessing on THIS HOUSE [White House], and on ALL that shall hereafter Inhabit it. May none but Honest and Wise Men ever rule under This Roof!

- John Adams

I've joked about every prominent man of my time, but I never met a man I didn't like.
- Will Rogers

Be in general virtuous, and you will be happy.
- Ben Franklin, Letter to John Alleyne, 1768

In reality there is perhaps no one of our natural passions so hard to subdue as pride. Disguise it, struggle with it, beat it down, stifle it, mortify it as much as one pleases, it is still alive, and will now and then peek out and show itself.
- Ben Franklin, Autobiography, 1771

For I agree with you that there is a natural aristocracy among men. The grounds of this are virtue and talents.
- Thomas Jefferson, October 28, 1813

Give up money, give up fame, give up science, give the earth itself and all it contains rather than do an immoral act. And never suppose that in any possible situation, or under any circumstances, it is best for you to do a dishonorable thing, however slightly so it may appear to you.
> - Thomas Jefferson, Letter to Peter Carr, 1785

Wish not so much to live long as to live well.
> - Ben Franklin, Poor Richard's Almanac, 1746

Although in the circle of his friends, where he might be unreserved with safety, he took a free share in conversation his colloquial talents were not above mediocrity, possessing neither copiousness of ideas, nor fluency of words. In public, when called on for a sudden opinion, he was unready, short and embarrassed.
> - Thomas Jefferson, about himself in a letter to Dr. Walter Jones, 1814

I have sometimes asked myself whether my country is the better for my having lived at all. I do not know that it is. I have been the instrument of doing the following things; but they would have been done by others; some of them, perhaps, a little better.
- Thomas Jefferson, 1800

I leave to others the sublime delights of riding in the storm...I have no ambition to govern men. It is a painful and thankless office.
- Thomas Jefferson, December 28, 1796

Amplification is the vice of modern oratory.
- Thomas Jefferson, Letter to David Harding, 1824

Work as if you were to live 100 Years, Pray as if you were to die tomorrow.
- Ben Franklin, Poor Richard's Almanac, 1757

I suppose, indeed, that in public life, a man whose political principles have any decided character and who has energy enough to give them effect must always expect to encounter political hostility from those of adverse principles.

> \- Thomas Jefferson, Letter to Richard M. Johnson, 1808

Determine never to be idle. No person will have occasion to complain of the want of time, who never loses any. It is wonderful how much may be done, if we are always doing. And that you may be always doing good, my dear, is the ardent prayer of yours affectionately.

> \- Thomas Jefferson, Letter to Martha Jefferson, 1787

Resolve to perform what you ought. Perform without fail what you resolve.

> \- Ben Franklin, Autobiography, 1771

Strive to be the greatest man in your country, and you may be disappointed. Strive to be your best and you may succeed: he may well win the race that runs by himself.
> - Ben Franklin, Poor Richard's Almanac, 1747

Have you something to do to-morrow; do it to-day.
> - Ben Franklin, Poor Richard's Almanac, 1742

I love the man that can smile in trouble, that can gather strength from distress, and grow brave by reflection.
> - Thomas Paine, The American Crisis, No. 1, 1776

Here comes the orator with his flood of words, and his drop of reason.
> - Ben Franklin, Poor Richard's Almanac, 1735

A dying man can do nothing easy.
- Ben Franklin, (After his daughter
asked him to move, 1790)

A fine genius in his own country is like gold in
the mine.
- Ben Franklin, Poor Richard's Almanac,
1733

I hope I shall possess firmness and virtue
enough to maintain what I consider the most
enviable of all titles, the character of an honest
man.
- George Washington

Facts are stubborn things; and whatever may
be our wishes, our inclination, or the dictates of
our passions, they cannot alter the state of facts
and evidence.
- John Adams, 1770

When we are planning for posterity, we ought to remember that virtue is not hereditary.
- Thomas Paine, Common Sense, 1776

I will hazard a prediction that, after the most industrious and impartial researchers, the longest liver of you all will find no principles, institutions or systems of education more fit in general to be transmitted to your posterity than those you have received from your ancestors.
- John Adams , Letter to the Young Men of Philadelphia, 1798

Labor to keep alive in your breast that little spark of celestial fire, called conscience.
- George Washington, The Rules of Civility, Circa 1748

Let your heart feel for the afflictions and distress of everyone, and let your hand give in proportion to your purse.
- George Washington

My observation is that whenever one person is found adequate to the discharge of a duty... it is worse executed by two persons, and scarcely done at all if three or more are employed therein.
- George Washington

The foolish and wicked practice of profane cursing and swearing is a vice so mean and low that every person of sense and character detests and despises it.
- George Washington

I was summoned by my country, whose voice I can never hear but with veneration and love.
- George Washington, First Inaugural Address, 1789

Good company will always be found much less expensive than bad.
- George Washington

Remember that it is the actions, and not the commission that make the officer, and that there is more expected from him, than the title.
    - George Washington

I hold the maxim no less applicable to public than to private affairs, that honesty is the best policy.
    - George Washington

Associate yourself with men of good quality if you esteem your own reputation; for 'tis better to be alone than in bad company.
    - George Washington

Be courteous to all, but intimate with few, and let those few be well tried before you give them your confidence. True friendship is a plant of slow growth, and must undergo and withstand the shocks of adversity before it is entitled to the appellation.
    - George Washington

To speak evil of any one, unless there is
unequivocal proof of their deserving it, is an
injury for which there is no adequate
reparation.
- George Washington

From thinking proceeds speaking; thence to
acting is often but a single step. But how
irrevocable and tremendous!
- George Washington

Nothing is a greater stranger to my breast, or a
sin that my soul more abhors, than that black
and detestable one, ingratitude.
- George Washington

When we assumed the Soldier, we did not lay
aside the Citizen.
- George Washington, Address to New
York Legislature, 1775

Require nothing unreasonable of your officers and men, but see that whatever is required be punctually complied with. Reward and punish every man according to his merit, without partiality or prejudice; hear his complaints; if well founded, redress them; if otherwise, discourage them, in order to prevent frivolous ones. Discourage vice in every shape, and impress upon the mind of every man, from the first to the lowest, the importance of the cause, and what it is they are contending for.
- George Washington

Citizens by birth or choice, of a common country, that country has a right to concentrate your affections. The name of AMERICAN, which belongs to you, in your national capacity, must always exalt the just pride of Patriotism, more than any appellation derived from local discriminations.
- George Washington, Farewell Address, 1796

CONGRESS

A local spirit will infallibly prevail much more in the members of Congress than a national spirit will prevail in the legislatures of the particular States.
- James Madison, Federalist No. 46

Such will be the relation between the House of Representatives and their constituents. Duty gratitude, interest, ambition itself, are the cords by which they will be bound to fidelity and sympathy with the great mass of the people.
- James Madison, Federalist No. 57, 1788

You have to pass the bill, so you can see what's in it.
- Speaker Nancy Pelosi, 2009

Laws are made for men of ordinary understanding and should, therefore, be construed by the ordinary rules of common sense. Their meaning is not to be sought for in metaphysical subtleties which may make anything mean everything or nothing at pleasure.
> - Thomas Jefferson, Letter to William Johnson, 1823

If the present Congress errs in too much talking, how can it be otherwise in a body to which the people send 150 lawyers, whose trade it is to question everything, yield nothing, & talk by the hour? That 150 lawyers should do business together ought not to be expected.
> - Thomas Jefferson, Autobiography, 1821

The house of representatives...can make no law which will not have its full operation on themselves and their friends, as well as the great mass of society. This has always been deemed one of the strongest bonds by which human policy can connect the rulers and the people together. It creates between them that communion of interest, and sympathy of sentiments, of which few governments have furnished examples; but without which every government degenerates into tyranny.
- James Madison, Federalist No. 57, 1788

The history of ancient and modern republics had taught them that many of the evils which those republics suffered arose from the want of a certain balance, and that mutual control indispensable to a wise administration. They were convinced that popular assemblies are frequently misguided by ignorance, by sudden impulses, and the intrigues of ambitious men; and that some firm barrier against these operations was necessary. They, therefore, instituted your Senate.
- Alexander Hamilton, To the New York Ratifying Convention, 1788

The injury which may possibly be done by defeating a few good laws, will be amply compensated by the advantage of preventing a number of bad ones.
> - Alexander Hamilton, Federalist No. 73, on the Veto Power, 1788

The natural cure for an ill-administration, in a popular or representative constitution, is a change of men.
> - Alexander Hamilton, Federalist No. 21, 1787

Remember, write to your congressman. Even if he can't read – write to him.
> - Will Rogers

I think I can say, and say with pride, that we have some legislatures that bring higher prices than any in the world.
> - Mark Twain, 1875

Loan sharks and interest hounds – I have addressed every form of organized graft in the United States – excepting Congress.
- Will Rogers

Can any of you seriously say the Bill of Rights could get through Congress today? It wouldn't even get out of committee.
- F. Lee Bailey

One hundred and seventy-three despots would surely be as oppressive as one.
- Federalist No. 48, 1788

Nothing has yet been offered to invalidate the doctrine that the meaning of the Constitution may as well be ascertained by the Legislative as by the Judicial authority.
- James Madison, Speech to Congress, 1789

THE CONSTITUTION

The basis of our political system is the right of
the people to make and alter their constitutions
of government. But the constitution which at
any time exists, until changed by an explicit
and authentic act of the whole people, is
sacredly obligatory upon all.
> - George Washington, Farewell Address,
> 1796

The only foundation of a free constitution, is
pure virtue, and if this cannot be inspired into
our people...they may change their rulers, and
the forms of government, but they will not
obtain a lasting liberty.
> - John Adams , Letter to Zabdiel Adams,
> 1776

The Constitution is the guide which I never will abandon.
>   - George Washington

A constitution founded on these principles introduces knowledge among the people, and inspires them with a conscious dignity becoming freemen.
>   - John Adams, Thoughts on
>   Government, 1776

Our Constitution was made only for a moral and religious people. It is wholly inadequate to the government of any other.
>   - John Adams, Address to the Military,
>   1798

Nothing has yet been offered to invalidate the doctrine that the meaning of the Constitution may as well be ascertained by the Legislative as by the Judicial authority.
>   - James Madison, Speech to Congress,
>   1789

Each State, in ratifying the Constitution, is considered as a sovereign body, independent of all others, and only to be bound by its own voluntary act. In this relation, then, the new Constitution will, if established, be a FEDERAL, and not a NATIONAL constitution.
- James Madison, Federalist No. 39, 1788

I acknowledge, in the ordinary course of government, that the exposition of the laws and Constitution devolves upon the judicial. But I beg to know upon what principle it can be contended that any one department draws from the Constitution greater powers than another in marking out the limits of the powers of the several departments.
- James Madison, Speech to Congress, 1789

[The Convention] thought it wrong to admit in the Constitution the idea that there could be men as property.
- James Madison, Records of the Convention, 1787

If it be asked what is to restrain the House of Representatives from making legal discriminations in favor of themselves and a particular class of the society? I answer, the genius of the whole system, the nature of just and constitutional laws, and above all the vigilant and manly spirit which actuates the people of America, a spirit which nourishes freedom, and in return is nourished by it.
>   - James Madison, Federalist No. 57, 1788

It is impossible for the man of pious reflection not to perceive in it [the Constitution] a finger of that Almighty hand which has been so frequently and signally extended to our relief in the critical stages of the revolution.
>   - James Madison, Federalist No. 37, 1788

A sacred respect for the constitutional law is the vital principle, the sustaining energy of a free government.
>   - Alexander Hamilton, Essay, American Daily Advertiser, 1794

Whatever may be the judgment pronounced on the competency of the architects of the Constitution, or whatever may be the destiny of the edifice prepared by them... that there never was an assembly of men, charged with a great and arduous trust, who were more pure in their motives, or more exclusively or anxiously devoted to the object committed to them.
- James Madison, circa 1835

You give me a credit to which I have no claim in calling me "the writer of the Constitution of the United States." This was not, like the fabled Goddess of Wisdom, the offspring of a single brain. It ought to be regarded as the work of many heads and many hands.
- James Madison, Letter to William Cogswell, 1834

Don't interfere with anything in the constitution. That must be maintained, for it is the only safeguard of our liberties.
- Abraham Lincoln, 1856

The aim of every political constitution is, or ought to be, first to obtain for rulers men who possess most wisdom to discern, and most virtue to pursue, the common good of the society; and in the next place, to take the most effectual precautions for keeping them virtuous whilst they continue to hold their public trust.
>   - Alexander Hamilton, Federalist No. 57, 1788

While the constitution continues to be read, and its principles known, the states, must, by every rational man, be considered as essential component parts of the union; and therefore the idea of sacrificing the former to the latter is totally inadmissible.
>   - Alexander Hamilton, To the New York Ratifying Convention, 1788

The Constitution is the sole source and guaranty of national freedom.
>   - Calvin Coolidge, 1924

[T]he Constitution ought to be the standard of construction for the laws, and that wherever there is an evident opposition, the laws ought to give place to the Constitution. But this doctrine is not deducible from any circumstance peculiar to the plan of convention, but from the general theory of a limited Constitution.
> - Alexander Hamilton, Federalist No. 81, 1788

[T]he present Constitution is the standard to which we are to cling...rejecting all changes but through the channel itself provides for amendments.
> - Alexander Hamilton, Letter to James Bayard, 1802

Our peculiar security is in the possession of a written Constitution. Let us not make it a blank paper by construction [reinterpretation].
> - Thomas Jefferson, Letter to Wilson Nicholas, 1803

I join cordially in admiring and revering the
Constitution of the United States, the result of
the collected wisdom of our country. That
wisdom has committed to us the important
task of proving by example that a government,
if organized in all its parts on the
Representative principle unadulterated by the
infusion of spurious elements, if founded, not
in the fears & follies of man, but on his reason,
on his sense of right, on the predominance of
the social over his dissocial passions, may be so
free as to restrain him in no moral right, and so
firm as to protect him from every moral wrong.
          - Thomas Jefferson, Letter to Amos
             Marsh, 1801

My construction of the constitution is very
different from that you quote. It is that each
department is truly independent of the others,
and has an equal right to decide for itself what
is the meaning of the constitution in the cases
submitted to its action; and especially, where it
is to act ultimately and without appeal.
          - Thomas Jefferson, Letter to Samuel
             Adams Wells, 1819

On every question of construction [interpretation] carry ourselves back to the time when the Constitution was adopted, recollect the spirit manifested in the debates and instead of trying what meaning may be squeezed out of the text or invented against it, conform to the probable one in which it was passed.
- Thomas Jefferson, Letter to William Johnson, 1823

The Constitution on which our Union rests, shall be administered by me [as President] according to the safe and honest meaning contemplated by the plain understanding of the people of the United States at the time of its adoption — a meaning to be found in the explanations of those who advocated [it].
- Thomas Jefferson, Letter to Mesrs. Eddy, Russel, Thurber, Wheaton and Smith, 1801

The Constitution is not neutral. It was designed to take the government off the backs of people.
- Justice William O. Douglas, 1980

The example of changing a constitution by
assembling the wise men of the state, instead
of assembling armies, will be worth as much to
the world as the former examples we had give
them. The constitution, too, which was the
result of our deliberation, is unquestionably
the wisest ever yet presented to men.
> - Thomas Jefferson, Letter to David
> Humphreys, 1789

Our constitution was not written in the sands
to be washed away by each wave of new
judges blown in by each successive political
wind.
> - Justice Hugo Black, 1970

Amendments to the constitution ought not to
be too frequently made...[if] continually
tinkered with it would lose all its prestige and
dignity, and the old instrument would be lost
sight of altogether in a short time.
> - President Andrew Johnson, 1866

The Constitution requires that Congress treat similarly situated persons similarly, not that it engage in gestures of superficial equality.
- Justice William Rehnquist, 1981

Recalling that it is a Constitution intended to endure for ages to come, we also remember that the founders wisely provided the means of endurance: Changes in the Constitution, when thought necessary, are to be proposed by Congress or conventions and ratified by the states. The Founders gave no such amending power to this Court.
- Justice Hugo Black, 1970

FINANCES

He that goes a borrowing goes a sorrowing.
- Ben Franklin, From his writings, 1758

You don't make the poor richer by making the rich poorer.
- Sir Winston Churchill, 1976

A penny saved is two pence clear.
- Ben Franklin, Poor Richard's Almanac, 1737

Having been poor is no shame, but being ashamed of it, is.
- Ben Franklin, 1749

He who is permitted by law to have no property of his own, can with difficulty conceive that property is founded in anything but force.
- Thomas Jefferson, January 26, 1788

Remember, that Time is Money.
- Ben Franklin, Advice to a Young Tradesman, 1748

As parents, we can have no joy…, as we are running the next generation into debt.
- Thomas Paine, Common Sense, 1776

FREE ENTERPRISE

I think all the world would gain by setting commerce at perfect liberty.
- Thomas Jefferson, July 7, 1785

If we can prevent the government from wasting the labors of the people, under the pretence of taking care of them, they must become happy.
- Thomas Jefferson, Letter to Thomas Cooper, 1802

No nation was ever ruined by trade, even seemingly the most disadvantageous.
- Ben Franklin, Principles of Trade, 1774

In our private pursuits it is a great advantage that every honest employment is deemed honorable. I am myself a nail-maker.
> - Thomas Jefferson, Letter to Jean Nicolas Démeunier, 1795

It should be our endeavor to cultivate the peace and friendship of every nation.... Our interest will be to throw open the doors of commerce, and to knock off all its shackles, giving perfect freedom to all persons for the vent to whatever they may choose to bring into our ports, and asking the same in theirs.
> - Thomas Jefferson, Notes on the State of Virginia, 1787

In this sense, the theory of the communists may be summed up in the single sentence: Abolition of private property.
> - Karl Marx, The Communist Manifesto, 1848

Here we are in a country with more wheat and more corn and more money in the bank, more cotton, more everything in the world – there's not a product you can name that we haven't got more of it than any country ever had on the face of the earth and yet we've got people starving. We'll hold the distinction of being the only nation in the history of the world that ever went to the poorhouse in an automobile.
- Will Rogers

The real democratic American ideal is , not that every man shall be on a level with every other man, but that every man shall have liberty to be what God made him, without hindrance.
- Henry Ward Beecher, 1887

The great depression, like most other periods of severe unemployment, was produced by government mismanagement rather than by any inherent instability of the private economy.
- Economist Milton Friedman, 1962

To take from one, because it is thought his own industry and that of his fathers has acquired too much, in order to spare to others, who, or whose fathers, have not exercised equal industry and skill, is to violate arbitrarily the first principle of association, the guarantee to everyone the free exercise of his industry and the fruits acquired by it.
> - Thomas Jefferson, Letter to Joseph Milligan, 1816

[A] wise and frugal government... shall restrain men from injuring one another, shall leave them otherwise free to regulate their own pursuits of industry and improvement, and shall not take from the mouth of labor the bread it has earned. This is the sum of good government.
> - Thomas Jefferson, First Inaugural Address, 1801

This gave me occasion to observe, that when Men are employed they are best contented.
> - Ben Franklin, Autobiography, 1771

The prosperity of commerce is now perceived
and acknowledged by all enlightened
statesmen to be the most useful as well as the
most productive source of national wealth, and
has accordingly become a primary object of its
political cares.
> - Alexander Hamilton, Federalist No. 12,
> 1787

If he does not bring a Fortune with him, he
must work and be industrious to live.
> - Ben Franklin, Those Who Would Move
> to America, 1784

Recession is when your neighbor loses his job.
Depression is when you lose yours.   And
recovery is when Jimmy Carter loses his.
> - Ronald Reagan, 1980

Repeal that [welfare] law, and you will soon
see a change in their manners. Monday and
Tuesday, will soon cease to be holidays. Six
days shalt thou labor, though one of the old
commandments long treated as out of date,
will again be looked upon as a respectable
precept; industry will increase, and with it
plenty among the lower people; their
circumstances will mend, and more will be
done for their happiness by inuring them to
provide for themselves, than could be done by
dividing all your estates among them.
- Ben Franklin, Letter to Collinson, 1753

It is also a truth, that if industry and labor are
left to take their own course, they will
generally be directed to those objects which are
the most productive, and this in a more certain
and direct manner than the wisdom of the
most enlightened legislature could point out.
- James Madison, Speech to Congress,
1789

I think the best way of doing good to the poor,
is not making them easy in poverty, but
leading or driving them out of it. In my youth I
traveled much, and I observed in different
countries, that the more public provisions were
made for the poor, the less they provided for
themselves, and of course became poorer. And,
on the contrary, the less was done for them, the
more they did for themselves, and became
richer.

> - Ben Franklin, On the Price of Corn and
> Management of the Poor, November
> 1766

GOD AND RELIGION

It is the duty of all men in society, publicly, and at stated seasons, to worship the SUPREME BEING, the great Creator and Preserver of the universe.
> - John Adams, Thoughts on Government, 1776

Let the poor and needy and oppressed of the earth, and those who want land, resort to the fertile plains of our western country, the second land of promise, and there dwell in peace, fulfilling the first and great commandment.
> - George Washington, Letter to David Humphreys, 1785

When you speak of God or his attributes, let it be seriously and with reverence.
- George Washington

The civil rights of none, shall be abridged on account of religious belief or worship, nor shall any national religion be established, nor shall the full and equal rights of conscience be in any manner, or on any pretext infringed.
- James Madison, Proposed amendment to the Constitution, given in a speech in the House of Representatives, 1789

The sacred rights of mankind are not to be rummaged for, among old parchments, or musty records. They are written, as with a sun beam, in the whole volume of human nature, by the hand of the divinity itself; and can never be erased or obscured by mortal power.
- Alexander Hamilton, The Farmer Refuted, 1775

[N]atural liberty is a gift of the beneficent Creator to the whole human race, and that civil liberty is founded in that; and cannot be wrested from any people, without the most manifest violation of justice.
- James Madison, The Farmer Refuted, 1775

Freedom prospers when religion is vibrant and the rule of law UNDER GOD is acknowledged.
- Ronald Reagan

It is the duty of every man to render to the Creator such homage and such only as he believes to be acceptable to him. This duty is precedent, both in order of time and in degree of obligation, to the claims of Civil Society.
- James Madison, Memorial and Remonstrance Against Religious Assessments, 1785

It is the duty of all nations to acknowledge the Providence of Almighty God, to obey His will, to be grateful for his benefits, and to humbly implore His protection and favor.
- George Washington

No man has a more perfect reliance on the all-wise and all powerful dispensations of the Supreme Being than I have, nor thinks his aid more necessary.
- George Washington

You do well to wish to learn the arts and ways of life, and above all, the religion of Jesus Christ. These will make you a greater and happier people than you are.
- George Washington

While we are zealously performing the duties of good citizens and soldiers, we certainly ought not to be inattentive to the higher duties of religion. To the distinguished character of Patriot, it should be our highest glory to add the more distinguished character of Christian.
- George Washington

As far as the strength of our reason and religion can carry us, a cheerful acquiescence to the Divine Will is what we are to aim.
- George Washington

It is with peculiar satisfaction I can say, that, prompted by a high sense of duty in my attendance on public worship, I have been gratified, during my residence among you, by the liberal and interesting discourses which have been delivered in your church.
   - George Washington

The propitious smiles of Heaven can never be expected on a nation that disregards the eternal rules of order and right, which Heaven itself has ordained.
      - George Washington, First Inaugural
         Address, 1789

Of all the dispositions and habits which lead to political prosperity, religion and morality are indispensable supports.
      - George Washington

It is impossible to rightly govern a nation without God and the Bible.
      - George Washington

The right to freedom being the gift of God
Almighty, it is not in the power of Man to
alienate this gift, and voluntarily become a
slave.
  - John Adams

No subject shall be hurt, molested, or
restrained, in his person, liberty, or estate, for
worshipping GOD in the manner most
agreeable to the dictates of his own conscience;
or for his religious profession or sentiments;
provided he doth not disturb the public peace,
or obstruct others in their religious worship.
    - John Adams

Let the pulpit resound with the doctrine and
sentiments of religious liberty. Let us hear of
the dignity of man's nature, and the noble rank
he holds among the works of God... Let it be
known that British liberties are not the grants
of princes and parliaments.
      - John Adams, Dissertation on the
      Canon and Feudal Law, 1765

The moment the idea is admitted into society that property is not as sacred as the laws of God, and that there is not a force of law and public justice to protect it, anarchy and tyranny commence; if `Thou shalt not covet' and `Thou shalt not steal' were not commandments of Heaven, they must be made inviolable precepts in every society before it can be civilized or made free.
- John Adams, A Defense of the American Constitution, 1787

But where is the King of America? I'll tell you friend, he reigns above, and does not make havoc of mankind like the royal brute of Britain.
- Thomas Paine, Common Sense, 1776

Let it be brought forth placed on the divine law, the word of God; let a crown be placed thereon, by which the world may know, that in America THE LAW IS KING.
- Thomas Paine, Common Sense, 1776

The reformation was preceded by the discovery of America, as if the Almighty graciously meant to open a sanctuary to the persecuted in future years, when home should afford neither friendship nor safety.
> - Thomas Paine, Common Sense, 1776

How many observe Christ's birthday! How few, his precepts! O! 'tis easier to keep Holidays than Commandments.
> - Ben Franklin, Poor Richard's Almanac, 1743

The deity...has constituted an eternal and immutable law, which is indispensably obligatory upon all mankind, prior to any human institution whatever. This is what is called the law of nature....Upon this law depend the natural rights of mankind.
> - Alexander Hamilton, The Farmer Refuted, 1775

Have we now forgotten that powerful friend [God]? Or do we imagine that we no longer need His assistance? I have lived, sir, a long time, and the longer I live, the more convincing proofs I see of this truth-that God governs in the affairs of men. And if a sparrow cannot fall to the ground without his notice, is it probable that an empire can rise without his aid?"
> - Ben Franklin, To the Constitutional Convention

No People can be bound to acknowledge and adore the invisible hand, which conducts the Affairs of men more than the People of the United States. Every step, by which they have advanced to the character of an independent nation, seems to have been distinguished by some token of providential agency.
> - George Washington, First Inaugural Address, 1789

Among the features peculiar to the political system of the United States, is the perfect equality of rights which it secures to every religious sect.
> - James Madison, Letter to Jacob de la Motta, 1820

We are teaching the world the great truth that
governments do better without Kings &
Nobles than with them. The merit will be
doubled by the other lesson that religion
flourishes in greater purity, without than with
the aid of government.
> - James Madison, Letter to Edward
>   Livingston, 1822

And can the liberties of a nation be thought
secure when we have removed their only firm
basis, a conviction in the minds of the people
that these liberties are the gift of God; that they
are not to be violated but with his wrath?
Indeed I tremble for my country when I reflect
that God is just: that his justice cannot sleep for
ever.
> - Thomas Jefferson, Notes on the State of
>   Virginia, Query 18, 1781

This new world has been the asylum for the
persecuted lovers of civil and religious liberty
from every part of Europe.
> - Thomas Paine, Common Sense, 1776

Reading, reflection and time have convinced me that the interests of society require the observation of those moral precepts...in which all religions agree.
> - Thomas Jefferson, Westmoreland County Petition, 1785

The God who gave us life, gave us liberty at the same time.
> - Thomas Jefferson, Summary View of the Rights of British America, August 1774

Without God there is no virtue because there is no prompting of the conscience. Without God there is a coarsening of the society. Without God democracy will not and cannot long endure. America needs God more than God needs America. If we ever forget that we are One Nation Under God, then we will be a Nation gone under.
> - Ronald Reagan, 1984

Believing with you that religion is a matter which lies solely between man and his God, that he owes account to none other for his faith or his worship, that the legislative powers of government reach actions only, and not opinions, I contemplate with sovereign reverence that act of the whole American people which declared that their legislature should "make no law respecting an establishment of religion, or prohibiting the free exercise thereof," thus building a wall of separation between church and State.
- Thomas Jefferson, To the Danbury Baptist Association, Connecticut, 1802

I consider the government of the United States as [prevented] by the Constitution from intermeddling with religious institutions, their doctrines, discipline, or exercises. This results not only from the provision that no law shall be made respecting the establishment or free exercise of religion, but from that also which reserves to the States the powers not delegated to the United States. Certainly, no power to prescribe any religious exercise or to assume authority in any religious discipline has been delegated to the General Government. It must then rest with the States.
- Thomas Jefferson, 1808

The establishment of civil and religious liberty
was the motive which induced me to the
field...and it now remains to be my earnest
wish and prayer, that the citizens of the United
States could make a wise and virtuous use of
the blessing placed before them.
  - George Washington, Letter to the
    Reformed German Congregation of
    New York City, 1783

Evil is powerless if the good are unafraid.
That's why the Marxist vision of man without
God must eventually be seen as an empty and
a false faith — the second oldest in the world
— first proclaimed in the Garden of Eden with
whispered words: 'Ye shall be as gods.' The
crisis of the Western world exists to the degree
in which it is indifferent to God.
  - Ronald Reagan, 1981

GOVERNMENT

On the distinctive principles of the
Government ... of the United States, the best
guides are to be found in... the Declaration of
Independence, as the fundamental act of union
of these states.
- James Madison, 1825

The ordaining of laws in favor of one part of
the nation, to the prejudice and oppression of
another, is certainly the most erroneous and
mistaken policy.
- Ben Franklin, Emblematical
Representations, Circa 1774

Government is not reason; it is not eloquent; it
is force. Like fire, it is a dangerous servant and
a fearful master.
- George Washington

They accomplished a revolution which has no parallel in the annals of human society. They reared the fabrics of governments which have no model on the face of the globe. They formed the design of a great confederacy, which it is incumbent on their successors to improve and perpetuate.
- James Madison, Federalist No. 14, 1787

One of the evils of democracy is, you have to put up with the man you elect, whether you want him or not.
- Will Rogers

Here sir, the people govern.
- Alexander Hamilton, Speech to the New York Ratifying Convention, 1788

[D]emocracies have ever been spectacles of turbulence and contention; have ever been found incompatible with personal security, or the rights of property; and have, in general, been as short in their lives as they have been violent in their deaths.
- James Madison, Federalist No. 10, 1787

The most sacred of the duties of a government [is] to do equal and impartial justice to all citizens.
> - Thomas Jefferson, Note in Destutt de Tracy, 1816

We may define a republic to be ... a government which derives all its powers directly or indirectly from the great body of the people, and is administered by persons holding their offices during pleasure for a limited period, or during good behavior.
> - James Madison, Federalist No. 39, 1788

I hope we have once again reminded people that man is not free unless government is limited. There's a clear cause and effect that's as neat and predictable as a law of physics: as government expands, liberty contracts.
> - President Ronald Reagan, 1989

The republican is the only form of government which is not eternally at open or secret war with the rights of mankind.
> - Thomas Jefferson, Letter to William Hunter, 1790

"We the people" tell the government what to do, it doesn't tell us. "We the people" are the driver – the government is the car. And we decide where it should go, and by what route, and how fast.
> - President Ronald Reagan, 1989

Every government degenerates when trusted to the rulers of the people alone. The people themselves, therefore, are its only safe depositories.
> - Thomas Jefferson, Notes on the State of Virginia, Query 14, 1781

Although a republican government is slow to move, yet when once in motion, its momentum becomes irresistible.
> - Thomas Jefferson, Letter to Francis C. Gray, 1815

If mankind were to resolve to agree in no institution of government, until every part of it had been adjusted to the most exact standard of perfection, society would soon become a general scene of anarchy, and the world a desert.
> - Alexander Hamilton, Federalist No. 65, 1788

Government is like a big baby – an alimentary canal with a big appetite on one end and no sense of responsibility at the other.
> - Ronald Reagan 1965

I think we have more machinery of government than is necessary, too many parasites living on the labor of the industrious.
> - Thomas Jefferson, Letter to William Ludlow, 1824

The people's government, made for the people, made by the people, and answerable to the people.
> - Daniel Webster, 1830

No government, any more than an individual, will long be respected without being truly respectable; nor be truly respectable, without possessing a certain portion of order and stability.

> - Alexander Hamilton, Federalist No. 62, 1788

It is not the function of our government to keep the citizen from falling into error; it is the function of the citizen to keep the government from falling into error.

> - Robert H Jackson, 1950

Why has government been instituted at all? Because the passions of men will not conform to the dictates of reason and justice without constraint.

> - Alexander Hamilton, Federalist No. 15, 1788

In all very numerous assemblies, of whatever
character composed, passion never fails to
wrest the scepter from reason. ... Had every
Athenian citizen been a Socrates, every
Athenian assembly would still have been a
mob.
- Alexander Hamilton, Federalist No. 55,
1788

In disquisitions [disputes] of every kind there
are certain primary truths, or first principles,
upon which all subsequent reasoning must
depend.
- Alexander Hamilton, Federalist No. 31,
1788

[If we] were...directed from Washington when
to sow, and when to reap, we should soon
want bread.
- Thomas Jefferson, Autobiography,
1821

In politics, as in religion, it is equally absurd to aim at making proselytes by fire and sword. Heresies in either can rarely be cured by persecution.

> \- Alexander Hamilton, Federalist No. 1, 1787

It seems to have been reserved to the people of this country, by their conduct and example, to decide the important question, whether societies of men are really capable or not of establishing good government from reflection and choice, or whether they are forever destined to depend for their political constitutions on accident and force.

> \- Alexander Hamilton, Federalist No. 1, 1787

It will be of little avail to the people...if the laws be so voluminous that they cannot be read, or so incoherent that they cannot be understood; if they be repealed or revised before they are promulgated, or undergo such incessant changes that no man, who knows what the law is today, can guess what it will be tomorrow.

> \- Alexander Hamilton, Federalist No. 62, 1788

That wise men have in all ages thought
government necessary for the good of
mankind; and, that wise governments have
always thought religion necessary for the well
ordering and well-being of society, and
accordingly have been ever careful to
encourage and protect the ministers of it,
paying them the highest public honors, that
their doctrines might thereby meet with the
greater respect among the common people.
- Ben Franklin, On that Odd Letter of
the Drum, 1730

Human government is more or less perfect as it
approaches nearer or diverges farther from the
imitation of this perfect plan of divine and
moral government.
- John Adams

A nation under a well regulated government
should permit none to remain uninstructed. It
is monarchical and aristocratic government
only that requires ignorance for its support.
- Thomas Paine, Rights of Man, 1792

Fear is the foundation of most governments; but it is so sordid and brutal a passion, and renders men in whose breasts it predominates so stupid and miserable, that Americans will not be likely to approve of any political institution which is founded on it.
> - John Adams, Thoughts on Government, 1776

Government is instituted for the common good, for the protection, safety, prosperity, and happiness of the people; and not for profit, honor, or private interest of any one man, family, or class of men.
> - John Adams, Thoughts on Government, 1776

Society in every state is a blessing, but government even in its best state, is but a necessary evil; in its worst state an intolerable one.
> - Thomas Paine, Common Sense, 1776

The people alone have an incontestable,
unalienable, and indefeasible right to institute
government; and to reform, alter, or totally
change the same, when their protection, safety,
prosperity, and happiness require it.
- John Adams, Thoughts on
Government, 1776

If, from the more wretched parts of the old
world, we look at those which are in an
advanced stage of improvement, we still find
the greedy hand of government thrusting itself
into every corner and crevice of industry, and
grasping the spoil of the multitude.
- Thomas Paine, Rights of Man, 1791

A dependence on the people is, no doubt, the
primary control on the government; but
experience has taught mankind the necessity of
auxiliary precautions.
- James Madison, Federalist No. 51

A republic, by which I mean a government in which the scheme of representation takes place, opens a different prospect and promises the cure for which we are seeking.
> - James Madison, Letter to William Hunter, 1790

Ambition must be made to counteract ambition. The interest of the man must be connected with the constitutional rights of the place. It may be a reflection on human nature that such devices should be necessary to control the abuses of government. What is government itself but the greatest of all reflections on human nature?
> - James Madison, Federalist No. 51, 1788

Justice is the end of government. It is the end of civil society. It ever has been and ever will be pursued until it be obtained, or until liberty be lost in the pursuit.
> - James Madison, Federalist No. 51, 1788

As there is a degree of depravity in mankind which requires a certain degree of circumspection and distrust: So there are other qualities in human nature, which justify a certain portion of esteem and confidence. Representative government presupposes the existence of these qualities in a higher degree than any other form.

> - James Madison, Federalist No. 55, 1788

Government is instituted to protect property of every sort; as well that which lies in the various rights of individuals, as that which the term particularly expresses. This being the end of government that alone is a just government which impartially secures to every man whatever is his own.

> - James Madison, Essay on Property, 1792

If men were angels, no government would be necessary. If angels were to govern men, neither external nor internal controls on government would be necessary. In framing a government which is to be administered by men over men, the great difficulty lies in this: you must first enable the government to control the governed; and in the next place, oblige it to control itself.

> - James Madison, Federalist No. 51, 1788

It has been said that all Government is an evil. It would be more proper to say that the necessity of any Government is a misfortune. This necessity however exists; and the problem to be solved is, not what form of Government is perfect, but which of the forms is least imperfect.
        - James Madison, 1833

Is there no virtue among us? If there be not, we are in a wretched situation. No theoretical checks-no form of government can render us secure. To suppose that any form of government will secure liberty or happiness without any virtue in the people, is a chimerical idea, if there be sufficient virtue and intelligence in the community, it will be exercised in the selection of these men, so that we do not depend on their virtue, or put confidence in our rulers, but in the people who are to choose them.
        - James Madison, Speech to Virginia Ratifying Convention, 1788

It is sufficiently obvious, that persons and property are the two great subjects on which Governments are to act; and that the rights of persons, and the rights of property, are the objects, for the protection of which Government was instituted. These rights cannot well be separated.

> - James Madison, Speech at the Virginia Convention, 1829

GUNS

No freeman shall be debarred the use of arms.
    - Thomas Jefferson, Draft Constitution
        for the State of Virginia, 1776

One loves to possess arms, though they hope
never to have occasion for them.
        - Thomas Jefferson, June 19, 1796

Firearms are second only to the Constitution in
importance; they are the peoples' liberty's
teeth.
        - George Washington

The very atmosphere of firearms anywhere
and everywhere restrains evil interference -
they deserve a place of honor with all that's
good.
- George Washington

A strong body makes the mind strong. As to
the species of exercises, I advise the gun. While
this gives moderate exercise to the body, it
gives boldness, enterprise and independence to
the mind. Games played with the ball, and
others of that nature, are too violent for the
body and stamp no character on the mind. Let
your gun therefore be your constant
companion of your walks.
- Thomas Jefferson, Letter to Peter Carr,
1785

Besides the advantage of being armed, which the Americans possess over the people of almost every other nation, the existence of subordinate governments, to which the people are attached and by which the militia officers are appointed, forms a barrier against the enterprises of ambition, more insurmountable than any which a simple government of any form can admit of.

- James Madison, Federalist No. 48, 1788

HUMANITY

The greatest thing we can do for the world is to be America.
> - Senator Marco Rubio, 2012 CPAC Conference

Mankind when left to themselves, are unfit for their own government.
> - George Washington

The cause of America is in a great measure the cause of all mankind.
> - Thomas Paine, Common Sense, 1776

We have no government armed with power capable of contending with human passions unbridled by morality and religion.
> - John Adams, Address to the Military, 1798

Those who expect to reap the blessings of freedom, must, like men, undergo the fatigues of supporting it.
> - Thomas Paine, The American Crisis, 1777

These are the times that try men's souls. The summer soldier and the sunshine patriot will, in this crisis, shrink from the service of his country; but he that stands it now, deserves the love and thanks of man and woman.
> - Thomas Paine, The American Crisis, 1776

Our cause is noble; it is the cause of mankind!
> - George Washington, Letter to James Warren, 1779

If there must be trouble, let it be in my day,
that my child may have peace.
>   - Thomas Paine, The American Crisis,
>   1776

The great principles of right and wrong are
legible to every reader; to pursue them
requires not the aid of many counselors. The
whole art of government consists in the art of
being honest. Only aim to do your duty, and
mankind will give you credit where you fail.
>   - Thomas Jefferson, A Summary View of
>   the Rights of British America, 1775

Every man who loves peace, every man who
loves his country, every man who loves liberty
ought to have it ever before his eyes that he
may cherish in his heart a due attachment to
the union of America and be able to set a due
value on the means of preserving it.
>   - James Madison, Federalist No. 41, 1788

The best service that can be rendered to a
Country, next to that of giving it liberty, is in
diffusing the mental improvement equally
essential to the preservation, and the
enjoyment of the blessing.
>- James Madison, Letter to Littleton
>Dennis Teackle, 1826

The American people are very generous people
and will forgive almost any weakness, with the
possible exception of stupidity.
>- Will Rogers

As long as the reason of man continues fallible,
and he is at liberty to exercise it, different
opinions will be formed.
>- James Madison, Federalist No. 10, 1787

'Tis the business of little minds to shrink; but
he whose heart is firm, and whose conscience
approves his conduct, will pursue his
principles unto death.

> - Thomas Paine, The American Crisis,
>   No. 1, 1776

LIBERTY

The preservation of the sacred fire of liberty
and the destiny of the republican model of
government are justly considered as deeply,
perhaps as finally, staked on the experiment
entrusted to the hands of the American people.
- George Washington, First Inaugural
Address, 1789

The right of freely examining public characters
and measures, and of free communication
among the people thereon ... has ever been
justly deemed the only effectual guardian of
every other right.
- James Madison, Virginia Resolutions,
1798

Nothing is more certainly written in the book
of fate than that these people are to be free.
- Thomas Jefferson, Autobiography,
1821

I suggest to you there is no left or right, only an
up or down. Up to the maximum of individual
freedom consistent with law and order, or
down to the ant heap of totalitarianism; and
regardless of their humanitarian purpose,
those who would sacrifice freedom for security
have, whether they know it or not, chosen this
downward path.
- Ronald Reagan, 1964

The fundamental source of all your errors,
sophisms and false reasoning is a total
ignorance of the natural rights of mankind.
Were you once to become acquainted with
these, you could never entertain a thought, that
all men are not, by nature, entitled to a parity
of privileges.
- James Madison, The Farmer Refuted,
1775

A free people [claim] their rights as derived from the laws of nature, and not as the gift of their chief magistrate.
>   - Thomas Jefferson, Rights of British America, 1774

The Declaration of Independence... [is the] declaratory charter of our rights, and the rights of man.
>   - Thomas Jefferson, Letter to Samuel Adams Wells, 1821

We have seen the mere distinction of color made in the most enlightened period of time, a ground of the most oppressive dominion ever exercised by man over man.
>   - James Madison, Constitutional Convention, 1787

Honor, justice, and humanity, forbid us tamely
to surrender that freedom which we received
from our gallant ancestors, and which our
innocent posterity have a right to receive from
us. We cannot endure the infamy and guilt of
resigning succeeding generations to that
wretchedness which inevitably awaits them if
we basely entail hereditary bondage on them.
- Thomas Jefferson, Declaration of the
Causes and Necessities of Taking Up
Arms, July 6, 1775

Liberty is not a means to a higher political end.
It is itself the highest political end.
- Lord Acton, 1877

Nothing then is unchangeable but the inherent
and unalienable rights of man.
- Thomas Jefferson, Letter to John
Cartwright, 1824

[T]o exclude foreign intrigues and foreign partialities, so degrading to all countries and so baneful to free ones; to foster a spirit of independence too just to invade the rights of others, too proud to surrender our own, too liberal to indulge unworthy prejudices ourselves and too elevated not to look down upon them in others; to hold the union of the States on the basis of their peace and happiness; to support the Constitution, which is the cement of the Union, as well in its limitations as in its authorities; to respect the rights and authorities reserved to the States and to the people as equally incorporated with and essential to the success of the general... as far as sentiments and intentions such as these can aid the fulfillment of my duty, they will be a resource which can not fail me.
- James Madison, Second Inaugural Address, 1813

I have sworn upon the altar of God, eternal hostility against every form of tyranny over the mind of man.
- Thomas Jefferson, Letter to Rev. Benjamin Rush September 1800

I have been happy... in believing that...
whatever follies we may be led into as to
foreign nations, we shall never give up our
Union, the last anchor of our hope, and that
alone which is to prevent this heavenly
country from becoming an arena of gladiators.
- Thomas Jefferson, Letter to Elbridge
Gerry, 1797

Equal and exact justice to all men, of whatever
persuasion, religious or political.
- Thomas Jefferson, First Inaugural
Address, 1801

Far from being a classless society, communism
is governed by an elite class as steadfast in its
determination to maintain its prerogatives as
any oligarchy in history.
- Robert F. Kennedy, 1964

Equal laws protecting equal rights — the best
guarantee of loyalty and love of country.
- James Madison, Letter to Jacob de la
Motta, 1820

One of the traditional methods of imposing statism or socialism on a people has been by way of medicine. It's very easy to disguise a medical program as a humanitarian project... James Madison in 1788 said: 'There are more instances of the abridgment of the freedom of the people by gradual and silent encroachment of those in power, than by violent and sudden usurpations.' We can say right now that we want no further encroachment on these individual liberties and freedoms. We do not want socialized medicine. Behind it will come other federal programs that will invade every area of freedom as we have known until, one day we will awake to find that we have socialism. And you and I are going to spend our sunset years telling our children and our children's children, what it once was like in America when men were free.
- Ronald Reagan, 1961

We should be unfaithful to ourselves if we should ever lose sight of the danger to our liberties if anything partial or extraneous should infect the purity of our free, fair, virtuous, and independent elections.
- John Adams, Inaugural Address, 1797

The spirit of resistance to government is so valuable on certain occasions, that I wish it to be always kept alive. It will often be exercised when wrong, but better so than not to be exercised at all. I like a little rebellion now and then. It is like a storm in the atmosphere.
- Thomas Jefferson, Letter to Abigail Adams 1787

To the press alone, checkered as it is with abuses, the world is indebted for all the triumphs which have been gained by reason and humanity over error and oppression.
- James Madison, Report on the Virginia Resolutions, 1798

While the last members were signing it Dr. Franklin looking towards the Presidents chair, at the back of which a rising sun happened to be painted, observed to a few members near him, that painters had found it difficult to distinguish in their art a rising from a setting sun.
- James Madison, Farrand's Records of the Federal Convention of 1787

This was the object of the Declaration of Independence. Not to find out new principles, or new arguments, never before thought of, not merely to say things which had never been said before; but to place before mankind the common sense of the subject, in terms so plain and firm as to command their assent, and to justify ourselves in the independent stand we are compelled to take. Neither aiming at originality of principle or sentiment, nor yet copied from any particular and previous writing, it was intended to be an expression of the American mind, and to give to that expression the proper tone and spirit called for by the occasion.
- Thomas Jefferson, Letter to Henry Lee, 1825

[The people] are in truth the only legitimate proprietors of the soil and government.
- Thomas Jefferson, Letter to Pierre Samuel Dupont de Nemours, 1813

[T]he flames kindled on the 4 of July 1776, have spread over too much of the globe to be extinguished by the feeble engines of despotism; on the contrary, they will consume these engines and all who work them.
- Thomas Jefferson, September 12, 1821

Tyranny, like hell, is not easily conquered; yet we have this consolation with us, that the harder the conflict, the more glorious the triumph.

> - Thomas Paine, The American Crisis, 1776

Is it not the glory of the people of America, that while they have paid a decent regard to the opinions of former times and other nations, they have not suffered a blind veneration for antiquity, for custom, or for names, to overrule the suggestions of their own good sense, the knowledge of their own situation, and the lessons of their own experience? To this manly spirit, posterity will be indebted for the possession, and the world for the example of the numerous innovations displayed on the American theatre, in favor of private rights and public happiness.

> - James Madison, Federalist No. 14, 1787

All eyes are opened, or opening, to the rights
of man. The general spread of the light of
science has already laid open to every view the
palpable truth, that the mass of mankind has
not been born with saddles on their backs, nor
a favored few booted and spurred, ready to
ride legitimately, by the grace of God.
  - Thomas Jefferson, Letter to Roger C.
    Weightman, 1826

No man in his senses can hesitate in choosing
to be free, rather than a slave.
  - Alexander Hamilton, A Full
    Vindication of the Measures of the
    Congress, etc., 1774

We must all hang together, or assuredly we
shall all hang separately.
  - Ben Franklin, (attributed), at the
    signing of the Declaration of
    Independence, 1776

Happily for America, happily, we trust, for the whole human race, they pursued a new and more noble course. They accomplished a revolution which has no parallel in the annals of human society.

- James Madison, Federalist No. 14, 1787

We fight not to enslave, but to set a country free, and to make room upon the earth for honest men to live in.

- Thomas Paine, The American Crisis, 1777

If by the liberty of the press were understood merely the liberty of discussing the propriety of public measures and political opinions, let us have as much of it as you please: But if it means the liberty of affronting, calumniating and defaming one another, I, for my part, own myself willing to part with my share of it, whenever our legislators shall please so to alter the law and shall cheerfully consent to exchange my liberty of abusing others for the privilege of not being abused myself.

- Ben Franklin, 1789

Every measure of prudence, therefore, ought to
be assumed for the eventual total extirpation of
slavery from the United States.... I have,
throughout my whole life, held the practice of
slavery in... abhorrence.
- John Adams

I can only say that there is not a man living
who wishes more sincerely than I do to see a
plan adopted for the abolition of slavery.
- George Washington

A little matter will move a party, but it must be
something great that moves a nation.
- Thomas Paine, The Rights of Man,
1792

Independence forever.
- (John Adams' last public words as a toast
for the celebration of the fiftieth
anniversary of the Declaration of
Independence)

If men through fear, fraud or mistake, should in terms renounce and give up any essential natural right, the eternal law of reason and the great end of society, would absolutely vacate such renunciation.

> - John Adams

[Independence Day] ought to be commemorated, as the Day of Deliverance by solemn Acts of Devotion to God Almighty. It ought to be solemnized with pomp and parade, with shows, games, sports, guns, bells, bonfires and illuminations [fireworks] from one end of this continent to the other from this time forward forever more.

> - John Adams , Letter to Abigail Adams, 1776

We are in the very midst of a revolution the most complete, unexpected and remarkable of any in the history of nations.

> - John Adams , Letter to William Cushing, 1776

Remember democracy never lasts long. It soon wastes, exhausts, and murders itself. There never was a democracy yet that did not commit suicide.
> - John Adams, Letter to John Taylor, 1814

The dons, the bashaws, the grandees, the patricians, the sachems, the nabobs, call them by what names you please, sigh and groan and fret, and sometimes stamp and foam and curse, but all in vain. The decree [Declaration of Independence] is gone forth, and it cannot be recalled, that a more equal liberty than has prevailed in other parts of the earth must be established in America.
> - John Adams, Letter to Patrick Henry, 1776

Liberty, when it begins to take root, is a plant of rapid growth.
> - George Washington, Letter to James Madison, 1788

I am well aware of the toil and blood and treasure, that it will cost us to maintain this Declaration, and support and defend these states. Yet through all the gloom I can see the rays of ravishing light and glory. I can see that the end is more than worth all the means.
- John Adams, to Abigail Adams, 1776

I must study politics and war that my sons may have liberty to study mathematics and philosophy. My sons ought to study mathematics and philosophy, geography, natural history and naval architecture, navigation, commerce and agriculture, in order to give their children a right to study painting, poetry, music, architecture, statuary, tapestry, and porcelain.
- John Adams, Letter to Abigail Adams, 1780

The Revolution was effected before the war commenced. The Revolution was in the minds and hearts of the people; a change in their religious sentiments, of their duties and obligations...This radical change in the principles, opinions, sentiments, and affections of the people was the real American Revolution.
- John Adams, Letter to H. Niles, 1818

But a Constitution of Government once changed from Freedom, can never be restored. Liberty, once lost, is lost forever.
- John Adams, Letter to Abigail Adams, 1775

Children should be educated and instructed in the principles of freedom.
- John Adams, Defense of the Constitution, 1787

Liberty must at all hazards be supported. We have a right to it, derived from our Maker. But if we had not, our fathers have earned and bought it for us, at the expense of their ease, their estates, their pleasure, and their blood.
- John Adams, Dissertation on the Canon and Feudal Law, 1765

Where liberty dwells, there is my country.
- Ben Franklin, (attributed), letter to Benjamin Vaughn, 1783

Freedom had been hunted round the globe;
reason was considered as rebellion; and the
slavery of fear had made men afraid to think.
But such is the irresistible nature of truth, that
all it asks, and all it wants, is the liberty of
appearing.
            - Thomas Paine, Rights of Man, 1791

He that would make his own liberty secure,
must guard even his enemy from oppression;
for if he violates this duty, he establishes a
precedent that will reach to himself.
            - Thomas Paine, Dissertation on First
                Principle of Government, 1791

They that can give up essential liberty to
purchase a little temporary safety, deserve
neither liberty nor safety.
            - Ben Franklin, Historical Review of
                Pennsylvania, 1759

Without freedom of thought there can be no such thing as wisdom; and no such thing as public liberty, without freedom of speech.
- Ben Franklin, Writing as Silence Dogood, 1722

It is a common observation here that our cause is the cause of all mankind, and that we are fighting for their liberty in defending our own.
- Ben Franklin, Letter to Samuel Cooper, 1777

In Europe, charters of liberty have been granted by power. America has set the example ... of charters of power granted by liberty. This revolution in the practice of the world, may, with an honest praise, be pronounced the most triumphant epoch of its history, and the most consoling presage of its happiness.
- James Madison, National Gazette Essay, 1792

The eyes of the world being thus on our country, it is put the more on its good behavior, and under the greater obligation also, to do justice to the tree of liberty by an exhibition of the fine fruits we gather from it.
- James Madison, Letter to James Monroe, 1824

What spectacle can be more edifying or more seasonable, than that of Liberty and Learning, each leaning on the other for their mutual & surest support?
- James Madison, Letter to W.T. Barry, 1822

There is a certain enthusiasm in liberty that makes human nature rise above itself, in acts of bravery and heroism.
- Alexander Hamilton, The Farmer Refuted, 1775

I will not believe our labors are lost. I shall not die without a hope that light and liberty are on a steady advance.
- Thomas Jefferson, September 12, 1821

I would rather be exposed to the inconveniences of attending too much liberty than those attending too small a degree of it.
    - Thomas Jefferson, Letter to Archibald Stewart, 1791

The boisterous sea of liberty is never without a wave.
    - Thomas Jefferson, Letter to Richard Rush, 1820

The natural progress of things is for liberty to yield and government to gain ground.
    - Thomas Jefferson, Letter to Edward Carrington, 1788

The tree of liberty must be refreshed from time to time with the blood of patriots and tyrants. It is its natural manure.
    - Thomas Jefferson, Letter to William Stephens Smith, 1787

Democracy and socialism have nothing in common but one word: equality. But notice the difference: while democracy seeks equality in liberty, socialism seeks equality in restraint and servitude.

    - Alexis de Tocqueville, 1848

I would remind you that extremism in the defense of liberty is no vice. And let me remind you that moderation in the pursuit of justice is not virtue.

    - Senator Barry Goldwater, 1964

MARRIAGE

A woman ... all beautiful and accomplished
will, while her hand and heart are not
promised, turn the heads and set the circle in
which she moves on fire. Let her marry, and
what is the consequence? The madness ceases
and all is quiet again. Why? Not because there
is any diminution in the charms of the lady,
but because there is an end of hope.
  - George Washington

I have always considered marriage as the most
interesting event of one's life, the foundation of
happiness or misery.
        - George Washington, Letter to Burwell
          Bassett, 1785

As long as Property exists, it will accumulate in Individuals and Families. As long as Marriage exists, Knowledge, Property and Influence will accumulate in Families.
- John Adams, Letter 1814

Keep your eyes wide open before marriage, half shut afterwards.
- Ben Franklin, Poor Richard's Almanac, 1738

The foundation of national morality must be laid in private families.
- John Adams, Diary entry, June 1778

The happy state of matrimony is...the cause of all good order in the world, and what alone preserves it from the utmost confusion...
- Ben Franklin, Rules and Maxims for Promoting Matrimonial Happiness, 1730

Harmony in the married state is the very first object to be aimed at.
> - Thomas Jefferson, Letter to Mary Jefferson Eppes, 1798

MILITARY

National defense is one of the cardinal duties
of a statesman.
> - John Adams , Letter to James Lloyd,
> 1815

America united with a handful of troops, or
without a single soldier, exhibits a more
forbidding posture to foreign ambition than
America disunited, with a hundred thousand
veterans ready for combat.
> - James Madison, Federalist No. 14, 1787

How could a readiness for war in time of peace
be safely prohibited, unless we could prohibit,
in like manner, the preparations and
establishments of every hostile nation?
> - James Madison, Federalist No. 41, 1788

It is a principle incorporated into the settled
policy of America, that as peace is better than
war, war is better than tribute.
> - James Madison, Letter to the Dey of
> Algiers, 1816

Let us recollect that peace or war will not
always be left to our option; that however
moderate or unambitious we may be, we
cannot count upon the moderation, or hope to
extinguish the ambition of others.
> - Alexander Hamilton, Federalist No. 34,
> 1788

To render the justice of the war on our part the
more conspicuous, the reluctance to commence
it was followed by the earliest and strongest
manifestations of a disposition to arrest its
progress. The sword was scarcely out of the
scabbard before the enemy was apprised of the
reasonable terms on which it would be re-
sheathed.
> - James Madison, Second Inaugural
> Address, 1813

Whatever enables us to go to war, secures our
peace.
> - Thomas Jefferson, Letter to James
> Monroe, 1823

To be prepared for war is one of the most
effectual means of preserving peace.
> - George Washington, First Annual
> Message, 1790

An army of asses led by a lion is vastly
superior to an army of lions led by an ass.
> - George Washington

Not all the treasures of the world, so far as I believe, could have induced me to support an offensive war, for I think it murder; but if a thief breaks into my house, burns and destroys my property, and kills or threatens to kill me, or those that are in it, and to "bind me in all cases whatsoever" to his absolute will, am I to suffer it?
> - Thomas Paine, The American Crisis, No. 1, 1776

What we obtain too cheap, we esteem too lightly: it is dearness only that gives every thing its value.
> - Thomas Paine, The American Crisis, No. 1, 1776

For the sake of humanity it is devoutly to be wished that...commerce would supersede the waste of war and the rage of conquest; and the swords might be turned into ploughshares, the spears into pruning-hooks, and as the Scripture expresses it, "the nations learn war no more."
> - George Washington

POWER

Arbitrary power is most easily established on
the ruins of liberty abused to licentiousness.
- George Washington, Circular to the
States, 1753

Public opinion sets bounds to every
government, and is the real sovereign in every
free one.
- James Madison, Public Opinion, 1791

All men having power ought to be distrusted
to a certain degree.
- James Madison, Speech at the
Constitutional Convention, 1787

The rights of neutrality will only be respected when they are defended by an adequate power. A nation, despicable by its weakness, forfeits even the privilege of being neutral.
> - Alexander Hamilton, Federalist No. 11, 1787

But ambitious encroachments of the federal government, on the authority of the State governments, would not excite the opposition of a single state, or of a few states only. They would be signals of general alarm... But what degree of madness could ever drive the federal government to such an extremity.
> - James Madison, Federalist No. 46, 1788

If the federal government should overpass the just bounds of its authority and make a tyrannical use of its powers, the people...take such measures to redress the injury done to the Constitution as the exigency may suggest and prudence justify.
> - James Madison, Federalist No. 33, 1788

Mere precedent is a dangerous source of authority.
- President Andrew Jackson, 1832

The fabric of American empire ought to rest on the solid basis of THE CONSENT OF THE PEOPLE. The streams of national power ought to flow from that pure, original fountain of all legitimate authority.
- James Madison, Federalist No. 22, 1787

Experience having long taught me the reasonableness of mutual sacrifices of opinion among those who are to act together for any common object, and the expediency of doing what good we can; when we cannot do all we would wish.
- Thomas Jefferson, Letter to John Randolph, 1803

The instrument by which it [government] must act are either the AUTHORITY of the laws or FORCE. If the first be destroyed, the last must be substituted; and where this becomes the ordinary instrument of government there is an end to liberty!
- James Madison, Tully, No. 3, 1794

[W]hen all government, domestic and foreign, in little as in great things, shall be drawn to Washington as the center of all power, it will render powerless the checks provided of one government on another.
- Thomas Jefferson, Letter to Charles Hammond, 1821

The construction applied...to those parts of the Constitution of the United States which delegate Congress a power...ought not to be construed as themselves to give unlimited powers, nor a part to be so taken as to destroy the whole residue of that instrument.
- Thomas Jefferson, Draft Kentucky Resolutions, 1798

I know no safe depository of the ultimate powers of the society but the people themselves; and if we think them not enlightened enough to exercise their control with a wholesome discretion, the remedy is not to take it from them, but to inform their discretion by education. This is the true corrective of abuses of constitutional power.
  - Thomas Jefferson, Letter to William Charles Jarvis, 1820

I consider the foundation of the Constitution as laid on this ground that 'all powers not delegated to the United States, by the Constitution, nor prohibited by it to the states, are reserved to the states or to the people.' To take a single step beyond the boundaries thus specially drawn around the powers of Congress, is to take possession of a boundless field of power, not longer susceptible of any definition.
  - Thomas Jefferson, Opinion on the Constitutionality of a National Bank, 1791

It would reduce the whole instrument to a single phrase, that of instituting a Congress with power to do whatever would be for the good of the United States; and as they would be the sole judges of the good or evil, it would be also a power to do whatever evil they please. Certainly no such universal power was meant to be given them. It [the Constitution] was intended to lace them up straightly within the enumerated powers and those without which, as means, these powers could not be carried into effect.
- Thomas Jefferson, Opinion on a National Bank, 1791

The legitimate powers of government extend to such acts only as are injurious to others. But it does me no injury for my neighbor to say there are twenty gods, or no god. It neither picks my pocket nor breaks my leg.
- Thomas Jefferson, Notes on the State of Virginia, Query 17, 1782

We established however some, although not all
its [self-government] important principles. The
constitutions of most of our States assert, that
all power is inherent in the people; that they
may exercise it by themselves, in all cases to
which they think themselves competent, (as in
electing their functionaries executive and
legislative, and deciding by a jury of
themselves, in all judiciary cases in which any
fact is involved,) or they may act by
representatives, freely and equally chosen; that
it is their right and duty to be at all times
armed.
- Thomas Jefferson, Letter to John
Cartwright, 1824

The Grecians and Romans were strongly
possessed of the spirit of liberty but not the
principle, for at the time they were determined
not to be slaves themselves, they employed
their power to enslave the rest of mankind.
- Thomas Paine, The American Crisis,
1778

A people who mean to be their own governors, must arm themselves with the power which knowledge gives.
>   - James Madison, Letter to W.T. Barry, 1822

An elective despotism was not the government we fought for; but one in which the powers of government should be so divided and balanced among the several bodies of magistracy as that no one could transcend their legal limits without being effectually checked and restrained by the others.
>   - James Madison, Federalist No. 48, 1788

In the first place, it is to be remembered, that the general government is not to be charged with the whole power of making and administering laws: its jurisdiction is limited to certain enumerated objects, which concern all the members of the republic, but which are not to be attained by the separate provisions of any.
>   - James Madison, Federalist No. 14, 1787

It will not be denied that power is of an encroaching nature and that it ought to be effectually restrained from passing the limits assigned to it. After discriminating, therefore, in theory, the several classes of power, as they may in their nature be legislative, executive, or judiciary, the next and most difficult task is to provide some practical security for each, against the invasion of the others.
- James Madison, Federalist No. 48, 1788

Wherever the real power in a government lies, there is the danger of oppression.
- James Madison, Letter circa 1788

The essence of Government is power; and power, lodged as it must be in human hands, will ever be liable to abuse.
- James Madison, Speech in the Virginia Constitutional Convention, 1829

There are more instances of the abridgment of the freedom of the people by gradual and silent encroachments of those in power than by violent and sudden usurpations.
> - James Madison, Speech to the Virginia Ratifying Convention, 1788

The powers delegated by the proposed Constitution to the federal government are few and defined. Those which are to remain in the State governments are numerous and indefinite.
> - James Madison, Federalist No. 45, 1788

Where an excess of power prevails, property of no sort is duly respected. No man is safe in his opinions, his person, his faculties, or his possessions.
> - James Madison, Essay in the National Gazette, 1792

[T]he government of the United States is a
definite government, confined to specified
objects. It is not like the state governments,
whose powers are more general. Charity is no
part of the legislative duty of the government.
- James Madison, Speech in the House of
Representatives, 1794

A fondness for power is implanted, in most
men, and it is natural to abuse it, when
acquired.
- James Madison, The Farmer Refuted,
1775

If Congress can do whatever in their discretion
can be done by money, and will promote the
general welfare, the government is no longer a
limited one, possessing enumerated powers,
but an indefinite one, subject to particular
exceptions.
- James Madison, Letter to Edmund
Pendleton, 1792

We have it in our power to begin the world over again.
> - Thomas Paine, The American Crisis, 1777

[T]he great security against a gradual concentration of the several powers in the same department consists in giving to those who administer each department the necessary constitutional means and personal motives to resist encroachment of the others.
> - James Madison, Federalist No. 10, 1787

The true principle of government is this: make the system complete in its structure; give a perfect proportion and balance to its parts; and the powers you give it will never affect your security.
> - James Madison, To the New York Ratifying Convention, 1788

What is to be the consequence, in case the Congress shall misconstrue this part [the necessary and proper clause] of the Constitution and exercise powers not warranted by its true meaning...the success of the usurpation will depend on the executive and judiciary departments, which are to expound and give effect to the legislative acts; and in a last resort a remedy must be obtained from the people, who can by the elections of more faithful representatives, annul the acts of the usurpers.

- James Madison, Federalist No. 44, 1788

The proposed Constitution, so far from implying an abolition of the State governments, makes them constituent parts of the national sovereignty, by allowing them a direct representation in the Senate, and leaves in their possession certain exclusive and very important portions of sovereign power. This fully corresponds, in every rational import of the terms, with the idea of a federal government.

- James Madison, Federalist No. 9, 1787

The regular distribution of power into distinct departments; the introduction of legislative balances and checks; the institution of courts composed of judges holding their offices during good behavior; the representation of the people in the legislature by deputies of their own election... They are means, and powerful means, by which the excellences of republican government may be retained and its imperfections lessened or avoided.

- James Madison, Federalist No. 9, 1787

THE STATES

State governments would clearly retain all the
rights of sovereignty which they before had,
and which were not, by that act,
EXCLUSIVELY delegated to the United States.
>   - Alexander Hamilton, Federalist No. 32,
>   1788

The operations of the federal government will
be most extensive and important in times of
war and danger; those of the State
governments, in times of peace and security.
>   - James Madison, Federalist No. 45, 1788

This balance between the National and State governments ought to be dwelt on with peculiar attention, as it is of the utmost importance. It forms a double security to the people. If one encroaches on their rights they will find a powerful protection in the other. Indeed, they will both be prevented from overpassing their constitutional limits by a certain rivalry, which will ever subsist between them.

> \- James Madison, To the New York
> Ratifying Convention, 1788

For the same reason that the members of the State legislatures will be unlikely to attach themselves sufficiently to national objects, the members of the federal legislature will be likely to attach themselves too much to local objects.

> \- James Madison, Federalist No. 47, 1788

The State governments possess inherent advantages, which will ever give them an influence and ascendancy over the National Government, and will forever preclude the possibility of federal encroachments. That their liberties, indeed, can be subverted by the federal head is repugnant to every rule of political calculation.
> - Alexander Hamilton, To the New York Ratifying Convention, 1788

Let the thirteen States, bound together in a strict and indissoluble Union, concur in erecting one great American system, superior to the control of all transatlantic force or influence, and able to dictate the terms of the connection between the old and the new world!
> - Alexander Hamilton, Federalist No. 11, 1787

There are certain social principles in human nature....we love our families more than our neighbors; we love our neighbors more than our countrymen in general. The human affections, like solar heat, lose their intensity as they depart from the center... On these principles, the attachment of the individual will be first and for ever secured by the State governments. They will be a mutual protection and support.

> \- Alexander Hamilton, To the New York Ratifying Convention, 1788

[T]he States can best govern our home concerns and the general government our foreign ones. I wish, therefore... never to see all offices transferred to Washington, where, further withdrawn from the eyes of the people, they may more secretly be bought and sold at market.

> \- Thomas Jefferson, Letter to Judge William Johnson, 1823

SUPREME COURT

One single object... [will merit] the endless gratitude of the society: that of restraining the judges from usurping legislation.
> - Thomas Jefferson, Letter to Edward Livingston, 1825

The standard of good behavior for the continuance in office of the judicial magistracy is certainly one of the most valuable of the modern improvements in the practice of government.
> - Alexander Hamilton, Federalist No. 78, 1788

[The Judicial Branch] may truly be said to have neither FORCE nor WILL, but merely judgment; and must ultimately depend upon the aid of the executive arm even for the efficacy of its judgments.
> \- Alexander Hamilton, Federalist No. 78, 1788

[T]he true key for the construction of everything doubtful in a law is the intention of the law-makers. This is most safely gathered from the words, but may be sought also in extraneous circumstances provided they do not contradict the express words of the law.
> \- Thomas Jefferson, Letter to Albert Gallatin, 1808

In the first place, there is not a syllable in the plan under consideration which directly empowers the national courts to construe the laws according to the spirit of the Constitution, or which gives them any greater latitude in this respect than may be claimed by the courts of every State.
> \- James Madison, Federalist No. 81, 1788

The germ of dissolution of our federal
government is in the constitution of the federal
judiciary; an irresponsible body, (for
impeachment is scarcely a scare-crow) working
like gravity by night and by day, gaining a
little today and a little tomorrow, and
advancing its noiseless step like a thief, over
the field of jurisdiction, until all shall be
usurped from the States, and the government
of all be consolidated into one.
> - Thomas Jefferson, Letter to Charles
> Hammond, 1821

A judiciary independent of a king or executive
alone, is a good thing; but independence of the
will of the nation is a solecism [blunder], at
least in a republican government.
> - Thomas Jefferson, Letter to Thomas
> Ritchie, 1820

Liberty can have nothing to fear from the
judiciary alone, but would have everything to
fear from its union with either of the other
departments.
> - James Madison, Federalist No. 78, 1788

The Constitution... is a mere thing of wax in the hands of the judiciary which they [apparently] may twist and shape into any form they please.

>   - Thomas Jefferson, Letter to Judge
>   Spencer Roane, 1819

[R]efusing or not refusing to execute a law to stamp it with its final character...makes the Judiciary department paramount in fact to the Legislature, which was never intended and can never be proper.

>   - James Madison, Letter to John Brown,
>   1788

The great object of my fear is the federal judiciary. That body, like gravity, ever acting, with noiseless foot, and unalarming advance, gaining ground step by step, and holding what it gains, is engulfing insidiously the special governments into the jaws of that which feeds them.

>   - Thomas Jefferson, Letter to Judge
>   Spencer Roane, 1821

The Judiciary...has no influence over either the sword or the purse; no direction either of the strength or of the wealth of the society, and can take no active resolution whatever. It may truly be said to have neither force nor will.
- James Madison, Federalist No. 78, 1788

The judiciary of the United States is the subtle corps of sappers and miners constantly working under ground to undermine the foundations of our confederated fabric. They are construing our constitution from a co-ordination of a general and special government to a general and supreme one alone.
- Thomas Jefferson, Letter to Thomas Ritchie, 1820

[T]he opinion which gives to the judges the right to decide what laws are constitutional and what not, not only for themselves, in their, own sphere of action, but for the Legislature and Executive also in their spheres, would make the Judiciary a despotic branch.
- Thomas Jefferson, Letter to Abigail Adams, 1804

Whoever attentively considers the different departments of power must perceive, that, in a government in which they are separated from each other, the judiciary, from the nature of its functions, will always be the least dangerous to the political rights of the Constitution; because it will be least in a capacity to annoy or injure them.

> \- James Madison, Federalist No. 78, 1788

At the establishment of our constitutions, the judiciary bodies were supposed to be the most helpless and harmless members of the government. Experience, however, soon showed in what way they were to become the most dangerous; that the insufficiency of the means provided for their removal gave them a freehold and irresponsibility in office...that these decisions, nevertheless, become law by precedent, sapping, by little and little, the foundations of the constitution, and working its change by construction, before any one has perceived that that invisible and helpless worm has been busily employed in consuming its substance.

> \- Thomas Jefferson, Letter to Monsieur A. Coray, 1823

Judiciary... working like gravity by night and by day, gaining a little today and a little tomorrow, and advancing its noiseless step like a thief, over the field of jurisdiction, until all shall be usurped.
> \- Thomas Jefferson, Letter to Charles Hammond, 1821

TAXES

No taxes can be devise which are not more or less inconvenient and unpleasant.
> - George Washington, Farewell Address, 1796

The most productive system of finance will always be the least burdensome.
> - James Madison, Federalist No. 39, 1788

We must not let our rulers load us with perpetual debt.
> - Thomas Jefferson, Letter to Samuel Kercheval, 1816

The multiplication of public offices, increase of expense beyond income, growth and entailment of a public debt, are indications soliciting the employment of the pruning knife.
- Thomas Jefferson, Letter to Spencer Roane, 1821

The principle of spending money to be paid by posterity, under the name of funding, is but swindling futurity on a large scale.
- Thomas Jefferson, Letter to John Taylor, 1816

An unlimited power to tax involves, necessarily, a power to destroy; because there is a limit beyond which no institution and no property can bear taxation.
- Chief Justice John Marshall, 1819

Our new Constitution is now established, and has an appearance that promises permanency; but in this world nothing can be said to be certain, except death and taxes.
- Ben Franklin, Letter to Jean-Baptiste Leroy, 1789

A just security to property is not afforded by that government, under which unequal taxes oppress one species of property and reward another species.
>   - James Madison, Essay on Property, 1792

There is not a more important and fundamental principle in legislation, than that the ways and means [taxes and expenditures] ought always to face the public engagements.
>   - James Madison, Speech in Congress, April 22, 1790

As to taxes, they are evidently inseparable from Government. It is impossible without them to pay the debts of the nation, to protect it from foreign danger, or to secure individuals from lawless violence and rapine.
>   - Alexander Hamilton, Address to the Electors of the State of New York, 1801

If duties are too high, they lessen the consumption; the collection is eluded; and the product to the treasury is not so great as when they are confined within proper and moderate bounds. This forms a complete barrier against any material oppression of the citizens by taxes of this class, and is itself a natural limitation of the power of imposing them.
> - Alexander Hamilton, Federalist No. 21, 1787

Excessive taxation will carry reason & reflection to every man's door, and particularly in the hour of election.
> - Thomas Jefferson, Letter to John Taylor, 1798

It is evident from the state of the country, from the habits of the people, from the experience we have had on the point itself, that it is impracticable to raise any very considerable sums by direct taxation.
> - Alexander Hamilton, Federalist No. 12, 1787

There is no part of the administration of government that requires extensive information and a thorough knowledge of the principles of political economy, so much as the business of taxation. The man who understands those principles best will be least likely to resort to oppressive expedients, or sacrifice any particular class of citizens to the procurement of revenue. It might be demonstrated that the most productive system of finance will always be the least burdensome.
- Alexander Hamilton, Federalist No. 35, 1788

Taxes should be continued by annual or biennial reactments [legislation], because a constant hold, by the nation, of the strings of the public purse is a salutary restraint from which an honest government ought not wish, nor a corrupt one to be permitted, to be free.
- Thomas Jefferson, Letter to John Wayles Eppes, 1813

Would it not be better to simplify the system of taxation rather than to spread it over such a variety of subjects and pass through so many new hands?
- Thomas Jefferson, 1784

If the [tax] system be established on basis of income, and his just proportion on that scale has been already drawn from every one, to step into the field of consumption, and tax special articles in that, as broadcloth or homespun, wine or whiskey, a coach or a wagon, is doubly taxing the same article. For that portion of income with which these articles are purchased, having already paid its tax as income, to pay another tax on the thing it purchased, is paying twice for the same thing; it is a grievance on the citizens who use these articles in exoneration of those who do not, contrary to the most sacred of the duties of a government, to do equal and impartial justice to all its citizens.

- Thomas Jefferson, Letter to Joseph Milligan, 1816

As on the one hand, the necessity for borrowing in particular emergencies cannot be doubted, so on the other, it is equally evident that to be able to borrow upon good terms, it is essential that the credit of a nation should be well established.

- Alexander Hamilton, Report on Public Credit, 1790

But with respect to future debt; would it not be wise and just for that nation to declare in the constitution they are forming, that neither the legislature, nor the nation itself can validly contract more debt, than they may pay within their own age, or within the term of 19 years.
- Thomas Jefferson, September 6, 1789

The same prudence which in private life would forbid our paying our own money for unexplained projects, forbids it in the dispensation of the public moneys.
- Thomas Jefferson, Letter to Shelton Gilliam, 1808

The great leading objects of the federal government, in which revenue is concerned, are to maintain domestic peace, and provide for the common defense.
- Alexander Hamilton, To the New York Ratifying Convention, 1788

A rigid economy [accounting] of the public contributions and absolute interdiction [elimination] of all useless expenses will go far towards keeping the government honest and unoppressive.
- Thomas Jefferson, Letter to Lafayette, 1823